MAKING WOODEN TOYS

12 Easy-to-Do Projects with Full-Size Templates

JAMES T. STASIO

Dover Publications, Inc.
New York

CONTENTS

Making Wooden Toys: 12 Easy-to-Do Projects with Full-Size Templates is a new work, first published by Dover Publications, Inc., in 1986.

Diagrams and templates rendered by David K. Andersen

Manufactured in the United States of America
Dover Publications, Inc., 31 East 2nd Street, Mineola, N.Y. 11501

Library of Congress Cataloging-in-Publication Data

Stasio, James T.
  Making wooden toys.

  Summary: Illustrated instructions for making twelve simple wooden toys including a freight train, cargo ship, helicopter, and others.
  1. Wooden toy making—Juvenile literature. [1. Toy making. 2. Woodwork. 3. Handi-craft] I. Title.
TT174.5.W6S73 1986   745.592   86-1466
ISBN 0-486-25112-8

INTRODUCTION

In recent years, toys have become more sophisticated. The computerized doll, the battery-operated truck, the remote-control tank have all been built to allow the child to sit, press a button, and watch the show. Yet the toy that is remembered most is the wooden one built by Dad or Grandpa for that special someone on that special day.

I have created this book to enable even relatively inexperienced hobbyists and craftsmen to derive a sense of accomplishment in fashioning wooden toys that will be cherished for generations. All of these toys can be made easily, using easy-to-find materials and simple tools. The book is designed so that no special instructions are necessary. For each project, a List of Materials tells you what you need, an Exploded Diagram and a photograph show how the pieces fit together, and exact-size templates enable you to cut the wood to precise dimensions. You may modify the dimensions I give to suit the tools you possess. Feel free to experiment as long as you are reasonably certain that your planned modifications will work.

Before beginning, you will need to choose a type of wood to work with. I recommend pine, for several reasons. It is inexpensive and available everywhere. It is easy to work with and readily takes nontoxic paints, stains, and oils. Finally, it finishes nicely, with a mellow color and smoothly flowing grain.

The toys in this book can be made using basic hand tools. Power tools will of course expedite your project, but they are not necessary. To make the wheels I used a portable electric drill (you may substitute a hand drill) with hole saws and mandrels measuring 1″, 1¼″, and 1⅞″. (The requirements for the projects are not strict. If you possess different-size hole saws, you may be able to make perfectly good toys with a few simple modifications.) Sand the outside of the wheels with #100 sandpaper. This will give the wheels a fine finish that will allow your toy to roll smoothly.

For simplicity's sake, I have limited the number of drill bits you will need to five: ⅛″, ¼″, ⅜″, ½″, and ¾″. With these, a drill to put them in, a workbench with a wood vise to hold your project while you are working on it, and the kinds of saws and screwdrivers commonly used for handywork around the house (a jigsaw or band saw will of course speed things up), in addition to the hole saws and mandrels mentioned above, you will have all the tools you need to complete any of these toys. Remember also to have on hand glue and several grades of sandpaper.

Some words of advice are in order at this point. Wherever possible, cut the wood so the grain runs lengthwise. Before gluing and finishing, sand the entire toy (sand always *with* the grain). Always begin with a rougher grade of sandpaper and work down to a finer grade. Remember, any time you spend in carefully sanding your toy will be rewarded by the pleasure you take in contemplating the fine finish and professional appearance of your work.

You may choose to paint any of these toys. Always use a nontoxic paint, as young children tend to put things in their mouth. Many companies offer a fine selection of colorful paints. Check the stock at your local crafts store. If you elect to paint your toy, the parts should be painted *before* gluing them together.

Instead of painting, you may apply a coat of varnish or even leave the wood unfinished. For a simple but effective finish, apply a light coat of linseed oil. This will lend the toy a golden color and emphasize the natural grain of the wood.

As you acquire experience working on these projects, you may wish to make a few alterations. Depending on your skill and desire, you may want to, say, add a smokestack, remove a dowel, or add a wheel. Feel free to make these changes or any that permit you to make maximum use of the tools you have on hand. The finished toy will then become a truly individual creation that you may give with pride.

HELICOPTER

(templates on Plate 1)

LIST OF MATERIALS

DESCRIPTION	NO. OF PIECES	SIZE
(A) Body Frame	1	9″ × 3″ × 1½″
(B) Stands	2	5½″ × ¾″ dowels
(C) Stand Posts	4	2″ × ½″ dowels
(D) Large Propeller	1	5″ × 1″ × ½″
(E) Small Propeller	1	3″ × ⅝″ × ½″
(F) Motor	1	1″ × ½″
(G) Screw	1	1½″-long #6 wood screw
(H) Screw	1	1″-long #6 wood screw
(I) Eyelets	2	¼″ metal eyelets

Note: The body frame (A) may be cut from a suitable length of two-by-four.

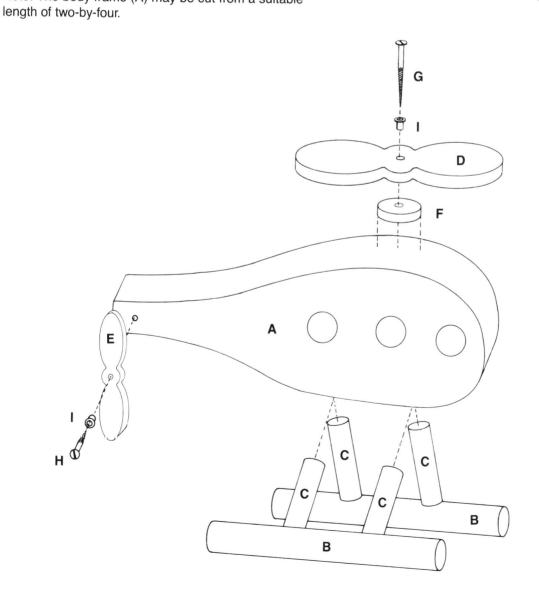

BIPLANE

(templates on Plates 2 and 3)

LIST OF MATERIALS

DESCRIPTION	NO. OF PIECES	SIZE
(A) Body Frame	1	$9\frac{1}{2}'' \times 2\frac{1}{4}'' \times \frac{3}{4}''$
(B) Wings	2	$8\frac{1}{2}'' \times 2'' \times \frac{1}{2}''$
(C) Tail	1	$4\frac{1}{2}'' \times 1\frac{1}{2}'' \times \frac{1}{2}''$
(D) Wheel Stand	1	$3'' \times 1'' \times \frac{3}{4}''$
(E) Propeller	1	$3'' \times \frac{5}{8}'' \times \frac{1}{2}''$
(F) Motor	1	$1'' \times \frac{1}{2}''$
(G) Prop Support	1	$1\frac{1}{2}'' \times \frac{1}{4}''$ dowel
(H) Wheels	2	$1'' \times \frac{3}{4}''$
(I) Tail Support	1	$1'' \times \frac{1}{4}''$ dowel
(J) Wing Struts	4	$3\frac{1}{2}'' \times \frac{1}{4}''$ dowels
(K) Axle	1	$5'' \times \frac{1}{4}''$ dowel

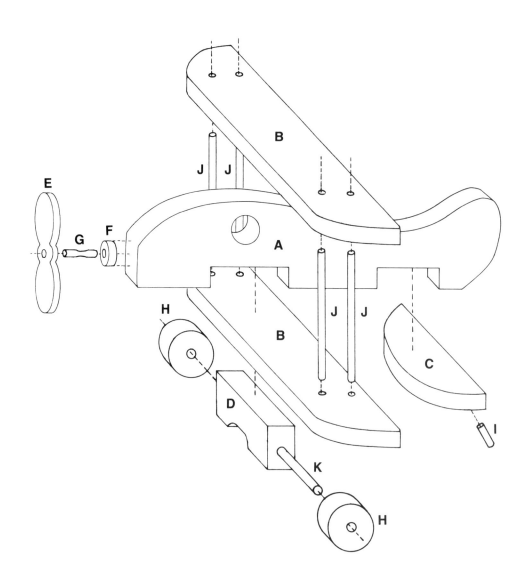

FREIGHT TRAIN

(templates on Plates 3 and 4)

LIST OF MATERIALS

DESCRIPTION	NO. OF PIECES	SIZE	DESCRIPTION	NO. OF PIECES	SIZE
(A) Train Cars	4	4″ × 2″ × ¾″	(I) Coal Car	1	3½″ × 2″ × 1½″
(B) Engine Cab	1	2″ × 1½″ × 1½″	(J) Oil Tank	1	3½″ × 1¼″ dowel
(C) Cab Roof	1	2″ × 1½″ × ½″	(K) Tank Cap	1	¼″ × ½″ dowel
(D) Smokestack	1	2″ × ½″ dowel	(L) Caboose	1	3½″ × 1½″ × 1½″
(E) Engine Light	1	1″ × ½″ dowel	(M) Caboose Cupola	1	1½″ × 1½″ × ½″
(F) Engine	1	1½″ × 1¼″ dowel	(N) Screw Eyes	3	#216½
(G) Wheels	16	1″ × ½″	(O) Screw Hooks	3	1¼″
(H) Axles	8	3½″ × ¼″ dowels			

Note: The engine cab (B), coal car (I), and caboose (L) may be cut from a suitable length of two-by-four.

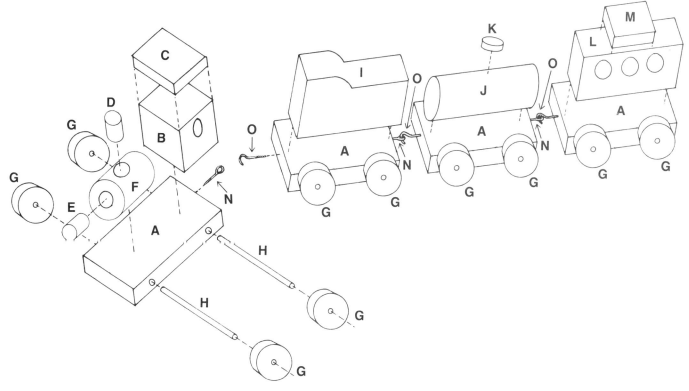

ROCKING HORSE AND SQUIRREL

(templates on Plate 5)

LIST OF MATERIALS

DESCRIPTION	NO. OF PIECES	SIZE
(A) Horse	1	5″ × 5½″ × ¾″
(B) Squirrel	1	4½″ × 4″ × ¾″
(C) Rockers	2	5½″ × 2″ × 1½″

Note: The rockers may be cut from a suitable length of two-by-four.

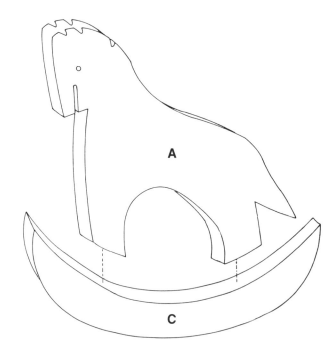

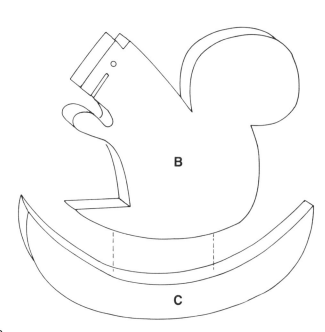

DOLL CRADLE

(templates on Plates 6 and 7)

LIST OF MATERIALS

DESCRIPTION	NO. OF PIECES	SIZE
(A) Base	1	10″ × 2½″ × ¾″
(B) Back and Front	2	4½″ × 4″ × ¾″
(C) Sides	6	10″ × ¼″ dowels
(D) Rockers	2	5″ × 1″ × ¾″

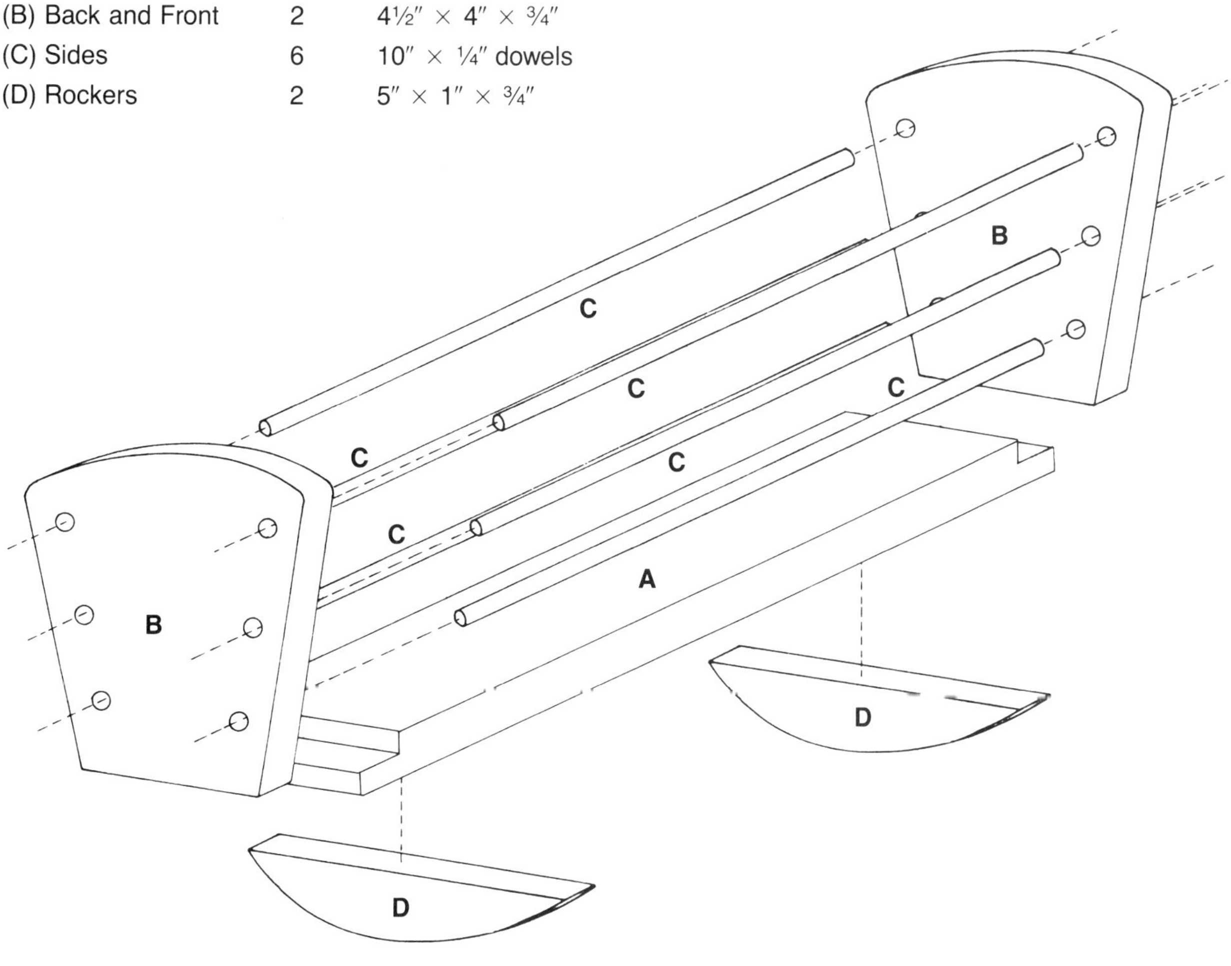

TRUCK BANK

(templates on Plates 7 and 8)

LIST OF MATERIALS

DESCRIPTION	NO. OF PIECES	SIZE
(A) Body Frame	1	7″ × 3″ × ¾″
(B) Sides	2	4½″ × 2½″ × ½″
(C) Front and Back	2	2″ × 2½″ × ½″
(D) Top	1	5″ × 3″ × ½″
(E) Wheels	4	1¾″ × ½″
(F) Bank Bottom	1	1¼″ × 1″ dowel (taper for fit)
(G) Axles	2	4½″ × ¼″ dowel
(H) Headlights	2	½″ × ¼″ dowels
(I) Radiator Cap	1	¼″ × ⁵⁄₁₆″ dowel
(J) Motor Block	1	2½″ × 1½″ × 2″

Note: The motor block (J) may be cut from a suitable length of two-by-four.

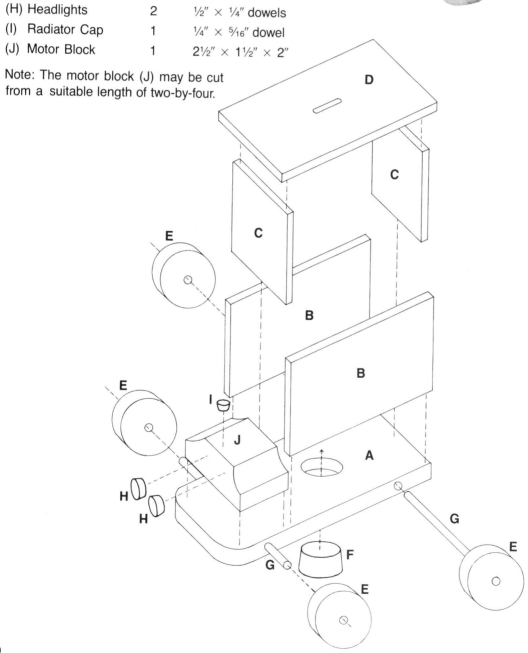

OIL TRUCK

(templates on Plate 9)

LIST OF MATERIALS

DESCRIPTION	NO. OF PIECES	SIZE	DESCRIPTION	NO. OF PIECES	SIZE
(A) Truck Cab	1	5″ × 2″ × 1½″	(E) Wheels	8	1″ × ½″
(B) Trailer	1	6″ × 2″ × ¾″	(F) Axles for Trailer	2	3½″ × ¼″ dowels
(C) Trailer Lock	1	1½″ × ½″ dowel	(G) Tank Cap	1	⅜″ × ½″ dowel
(D) Tank	1	4″ × 1¼″ dowel	(H) Axles for Cab	2	3″ × ¼″ dowels

Note: The truck cab (A) may be cut from a suitable length of two-by-four.

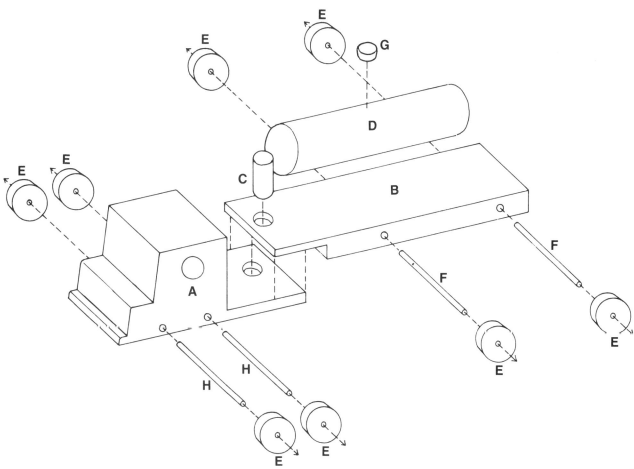

DESTROYER

(templates on Plate 10)

LIST OF MATERIALS

DESCRIPTION	NO. OF PIECES	SIZE
(A) Ship's Hull	1	9″ × 3½″ × ¾″
(B) Bridge	1	3″ × 2½″ × ¾″
(C) Bridge Cabin	1	2″ × 1″ × ¾″
(D) Gun Turrets	2	1″ × 1½″
(E) Turret Guns	2	1″ × ⅛″ dowels
(F) Spotlight	1	¼″ × ¼″ dowel
(G) Wheels	4	1″ × ¾″
(H) Axles	2	5½″ × ¼″ dowels
(I) Screws	2	1″-long #6 wood screws
(J) Screw Eye	1	#216½
(K) Eyelets	2	¼″ metal
(L) Smokestack	1	2″ × ¾″ dowel

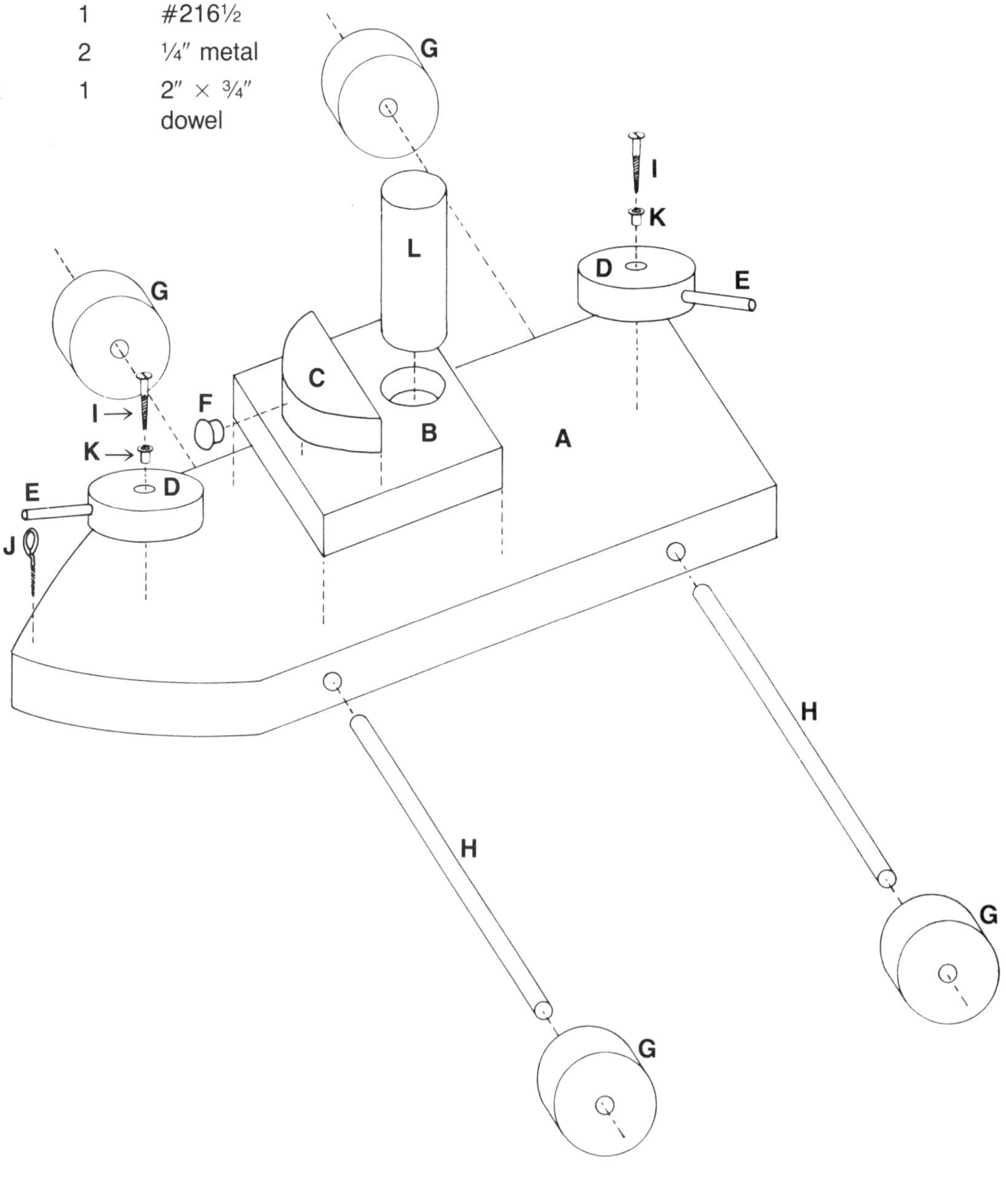

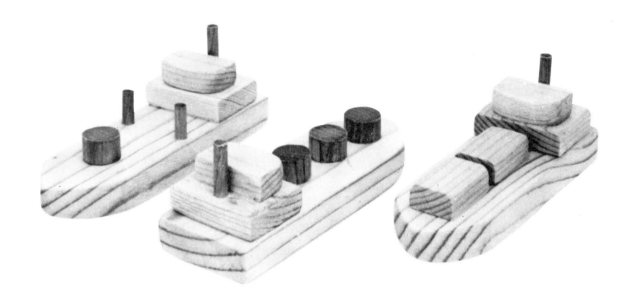

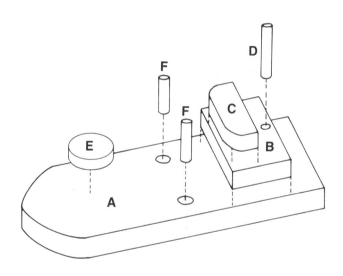

CARGO SHIPS

(templates on Plate 11)

LIST OF MATERIALS

DESCRIPTION	NO. OF PIECES	SIZE
(A) Ships' Hulls	3	6″ × 2″ × ¾″
(B) Bridges	3	2″ × 1½″ × ½″
(C) Bridge Cabins	3	1½″ × 1″ × ½″
(D) Smoke Stacks	3	1½″ × ¼″ dowels
(E) Cargo Hatches	4	½″ × ¾″ dowels
(F) Winches	2	1″ × ¼″ dowels
(G) Containers	2	1½″ × 1″ × 1½″

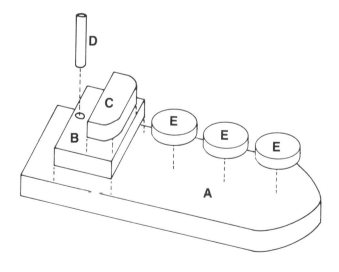

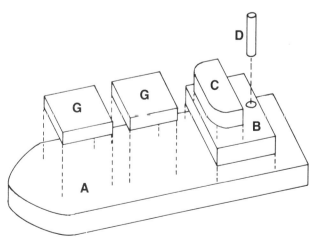

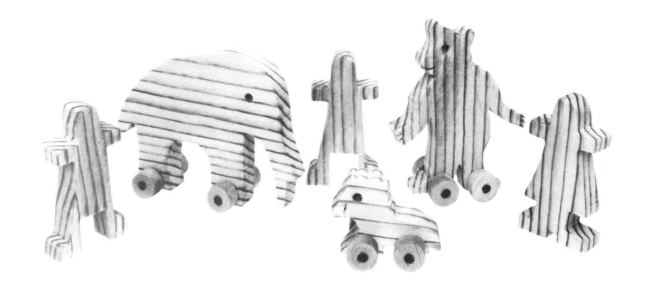

CIRCUS ANIMALS AND ACROBATS

(templates on Plates 12 and 13)

LIST OF MATERIALS

DESCRIPTION	NO. OF PIECES	SIZE
(A) Elephant	1	6″ × 4½″ × ¾″
(B) Lion	1	3″ × 2¼″ × ¾″
(C) Bear	1	5″ × 4″ × ¾″
(D) Acrobats (Male)	2	4″ × 2½″ × ¾″
(E) Acrobat (Female)	1	4″ × 2″ × ¾″
(F) Axles	6	2″ × ¼″ dowels
(G) Wheels	12	1″ × ½″

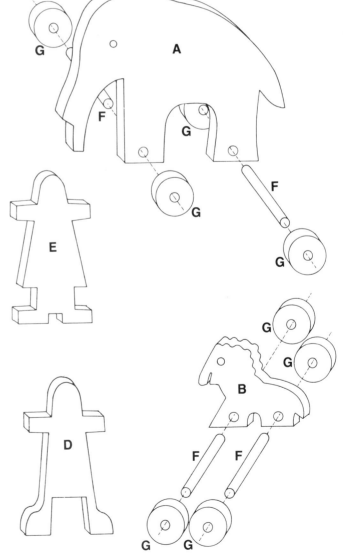

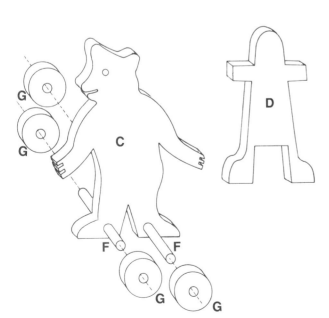

WORK TRUCK

(templates on Plate 14)

LIST OF MATERIALS

DESCRIPTION	NO. OF PIECES	SIZE
(A) Truck Frame	1	$8'' \times 3\frac{1}{2}'' \times 1\frac{1}{2}''$
(B) Cab	1	$3\frac{1}{2}'' \times 2'' \times 1\frac{1}{2}''$
(C) Sides	2	$3\frac{1}{2}'' \times 1'' \times \frac{1}{2}''$
(D) Wheels	4	$1\frac{3}{4}'' \times \frac{3}{4}''$
(E) Axles	2	$5\frac{1}{2}'' \times \frac{1}{4}''$ dowels
(F) Headlights	2	$\frac{1}{4}'' \times \frac{1}{2}''$ dowels
(G) Lights for Cab and Tail	4	$\frac{1}{4}'' \times \frac{1}{4}''$ dowels

Note: The truck frame (A) and cab (B) may be cut from a suitable length of two-by-four.

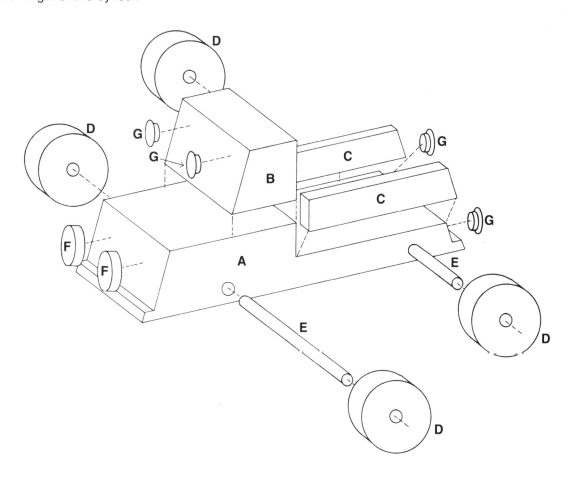

FIGHTER PLANE

(templates on Plate 15)

LIST OF MATERIALS

DESCRIPTION	NO. OF PIECES	SIZE	DESCRIPTION	NO. OF PIECES	SIZE
(A) Body Frame	1	9¼″ × 2¼″ × ¾″	(G) Motor	1	¾″ × ½″
(B) Wing	1	8½″ × 2″ × ¾″	(H) Axle	1	5″ × ¼″ dowel
(C) Tail	1	4½″ × 1½″ × ¾″	(I) Prop Support	1	1½″ × ¼″ dowel
(D) Wheel Stand	1	3″ × 1″ × ¾″	(J) Tail Support	1	1″ × ¼″ dowel
(E) Propeller	1	3″ × ⅝″ × ½″	(K) Guns	2	1½″ × ⅛″ dowels
(F) Wheels	2	1″ × ¾″			

Note: The center of the prop support (I) should be sanded to allow the propeller to spin freely.

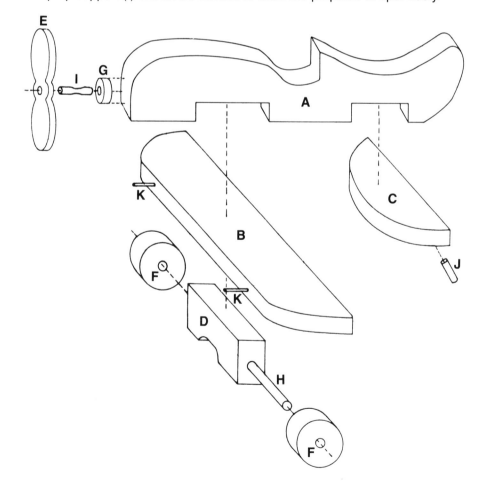

HELICOPTER

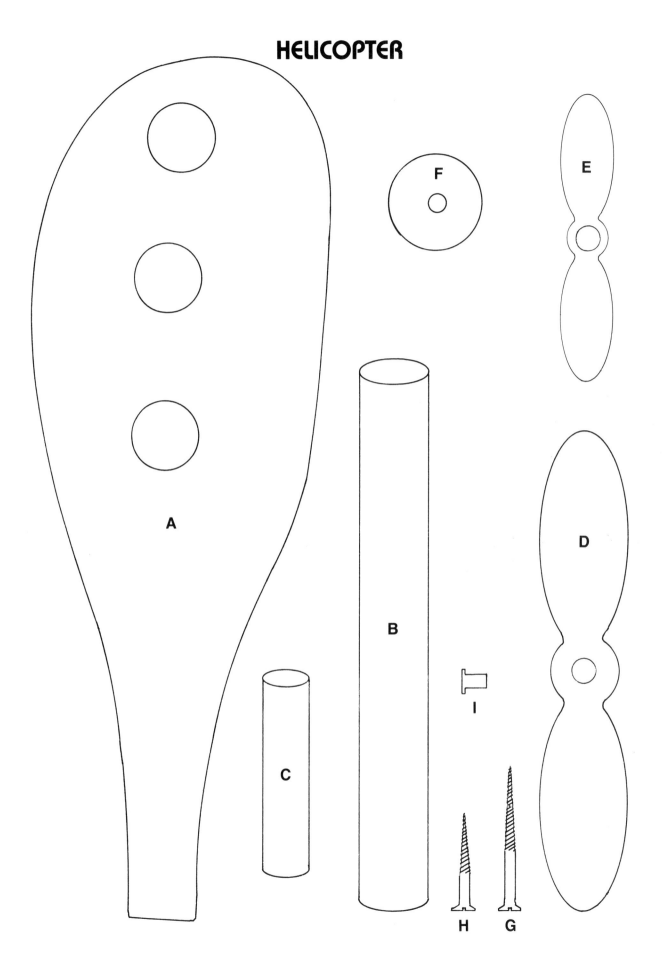

Plate 1

BIPLANE

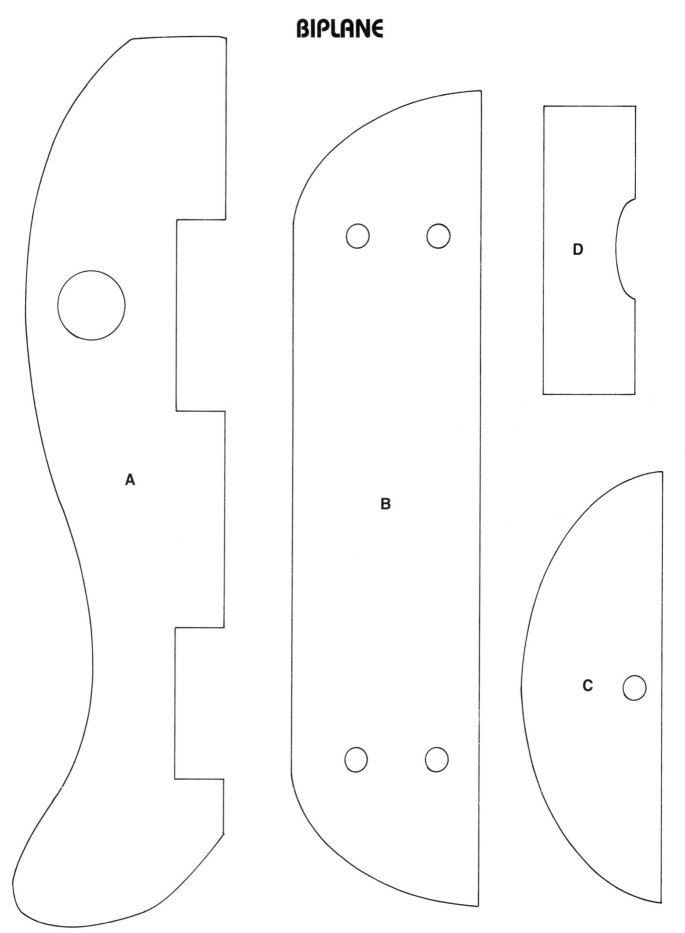

A

B

C

D

Plate 2

BIPLANE

FREIGHT TRAIN

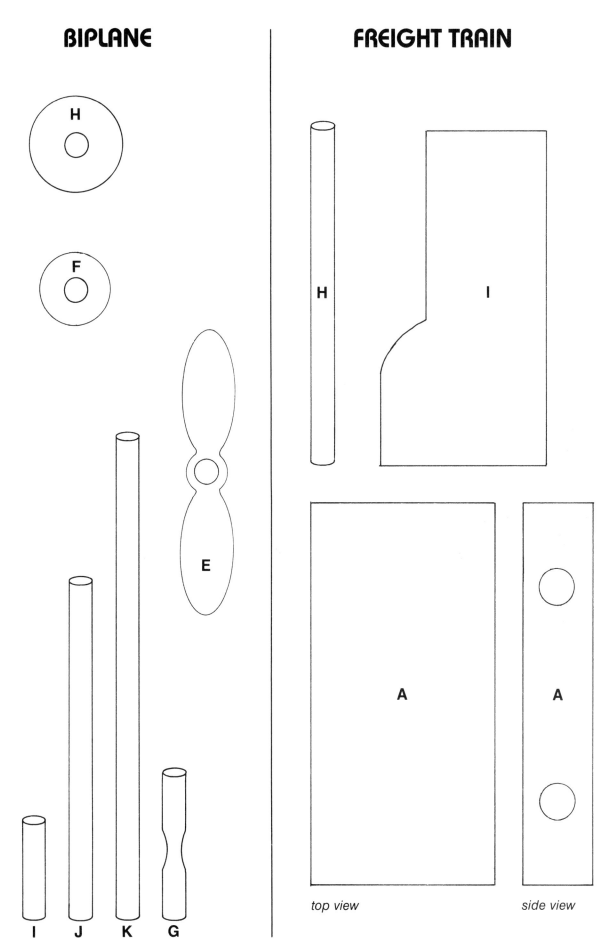

top view

side view

Plate 3

FREIGHT TRAIN

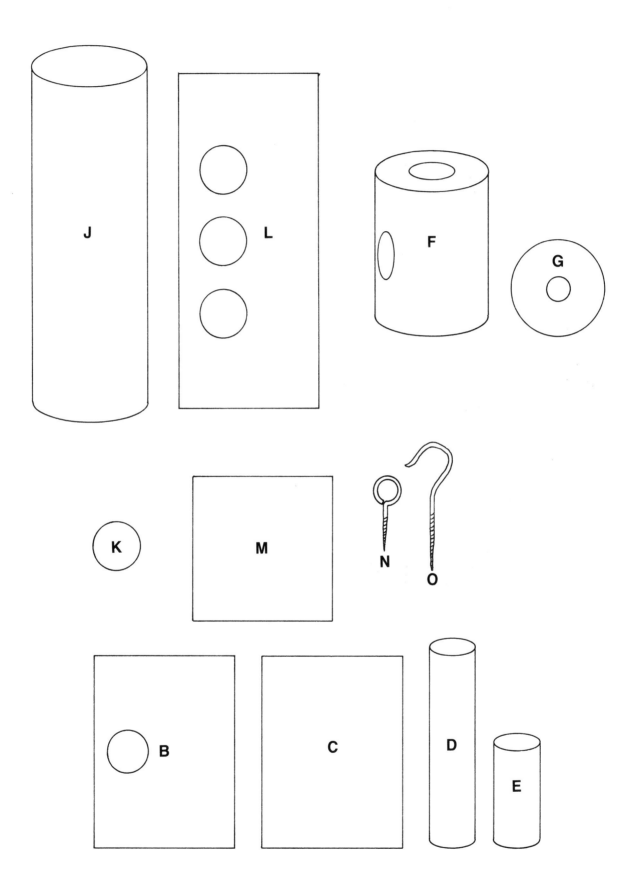

Plate 4

ROCKING HORSE

A

C

SQUIRREL

B

Plate 5

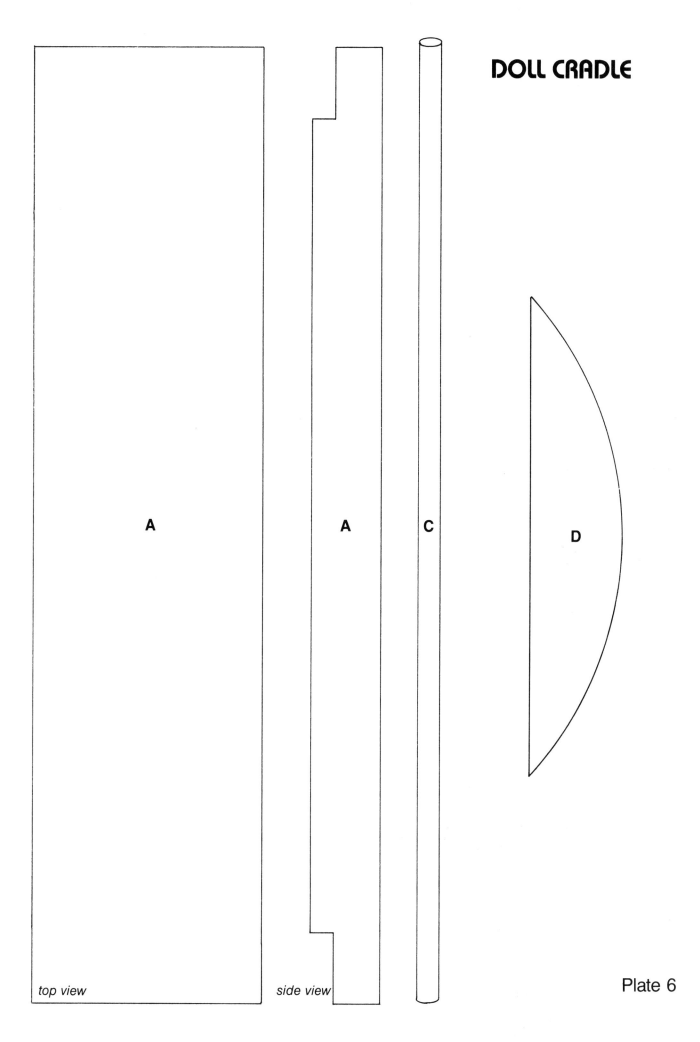

DOLL CRADLE

A

top view

A

side view

C

D

Plate 6

DOLL CRADLE

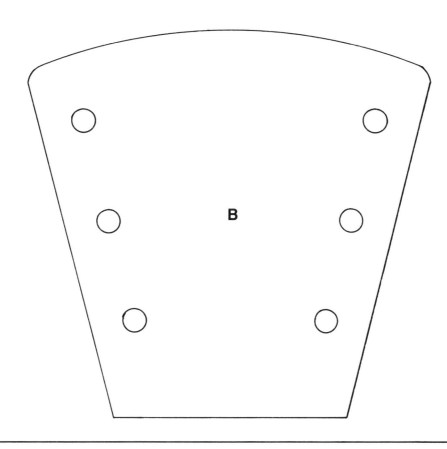

B

TRUCK BANK

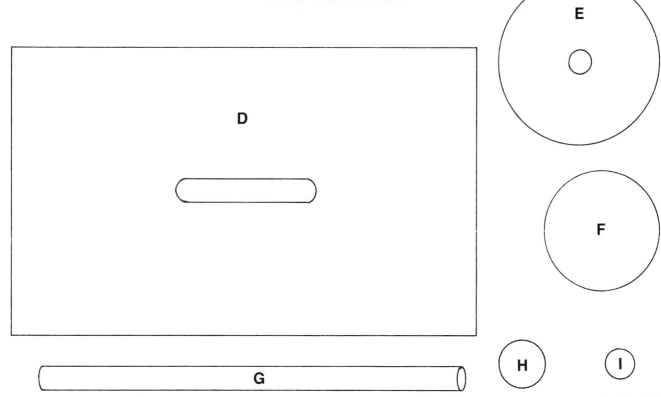

D

E

F

G

H

I

Plate 7

TRUCK BANK

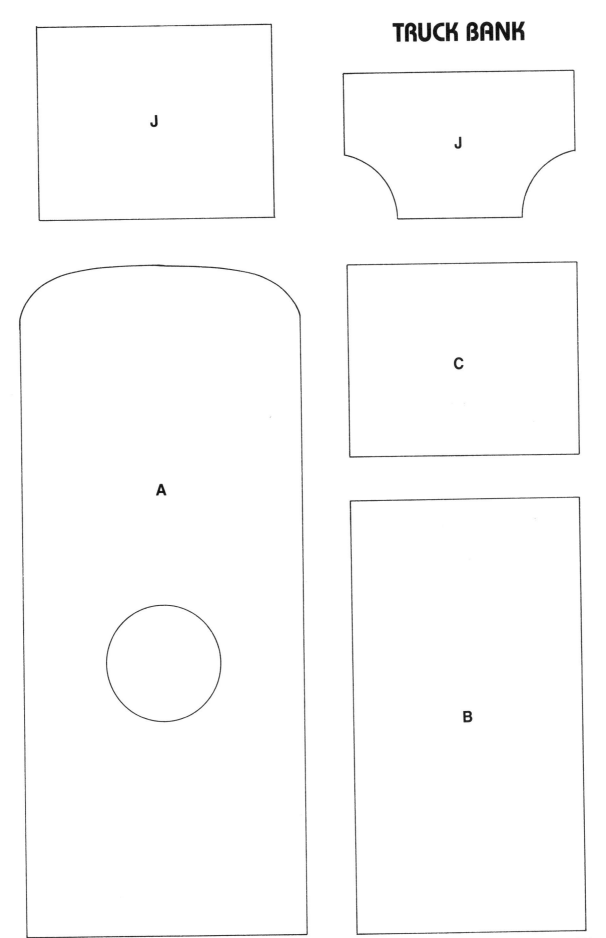

Plate 8

OIL TRUCK

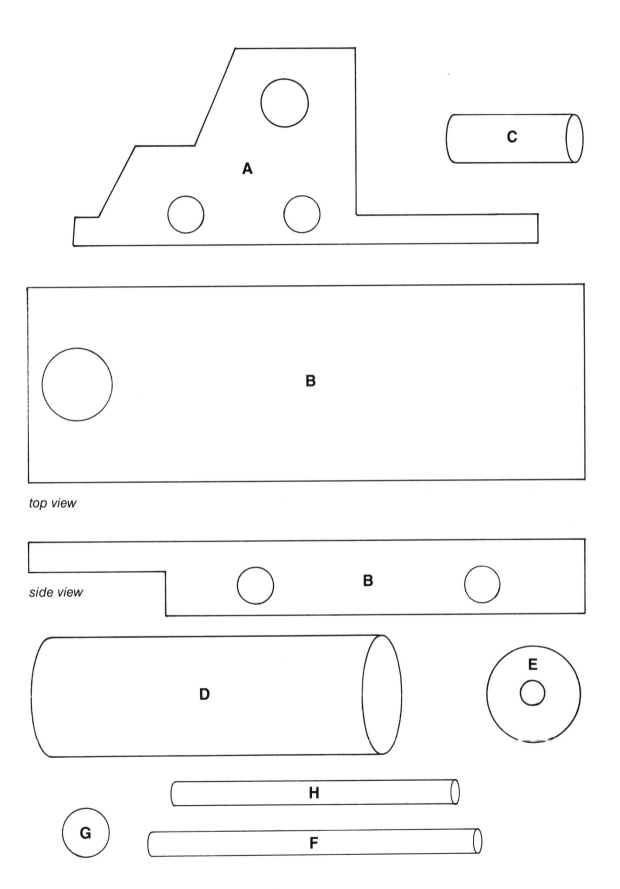

top view

side view

Plate 9

DESTROYER

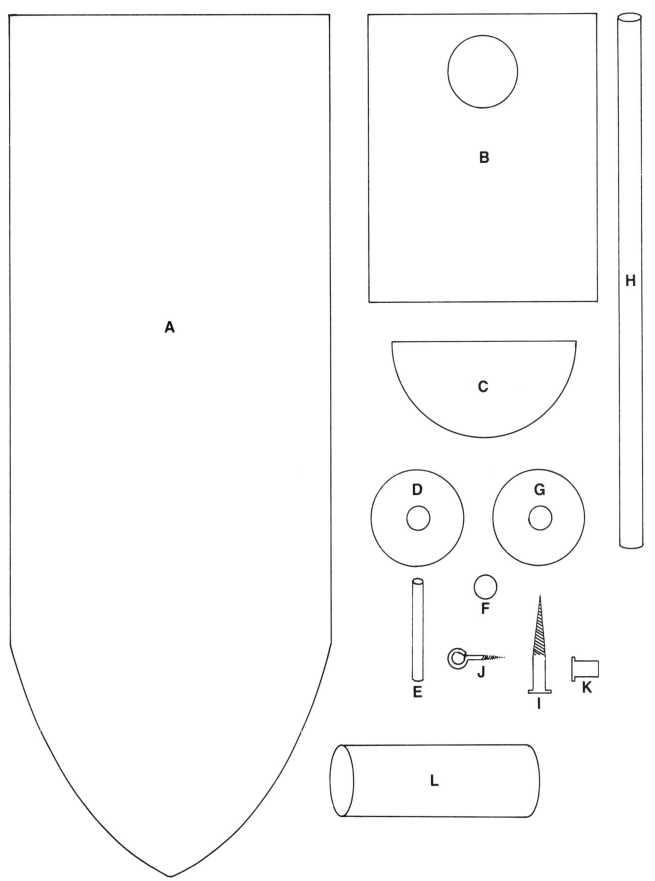

A

B

C

D

G

E

F

I

J

K

H

L

Plate 10

CARGO SHIPS

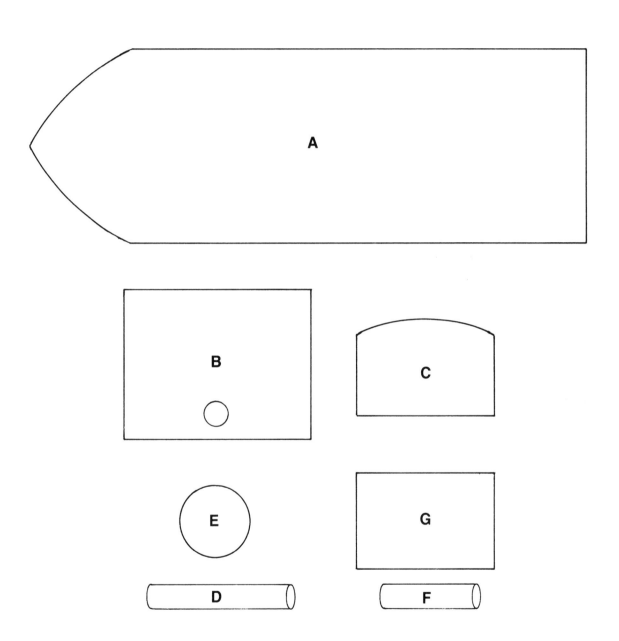

Plate 11

CIRCUS ANIMALS AND ACROBATS

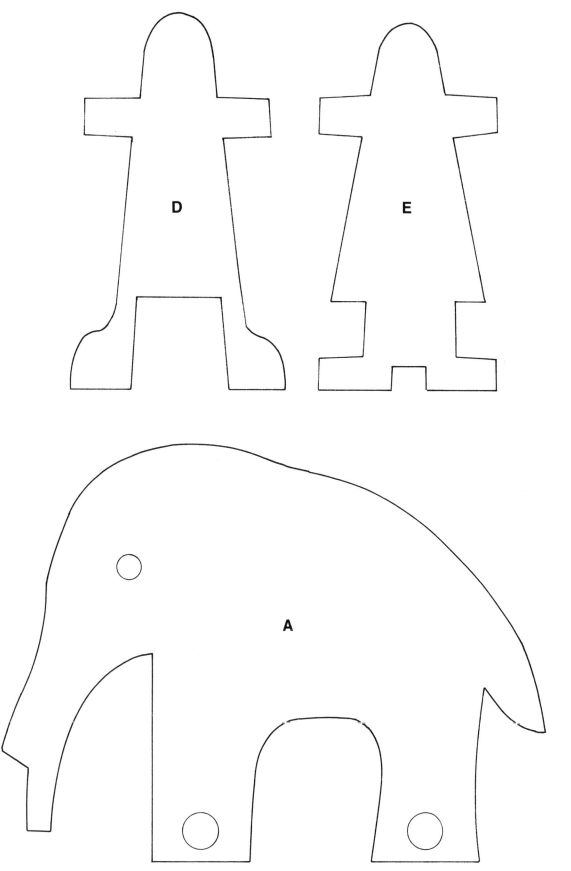

D

E

A

Plate 12

CIRCUS ANIMALS AND ACROBATS

B

C

F

G

Plate 13

WORK TRUCK

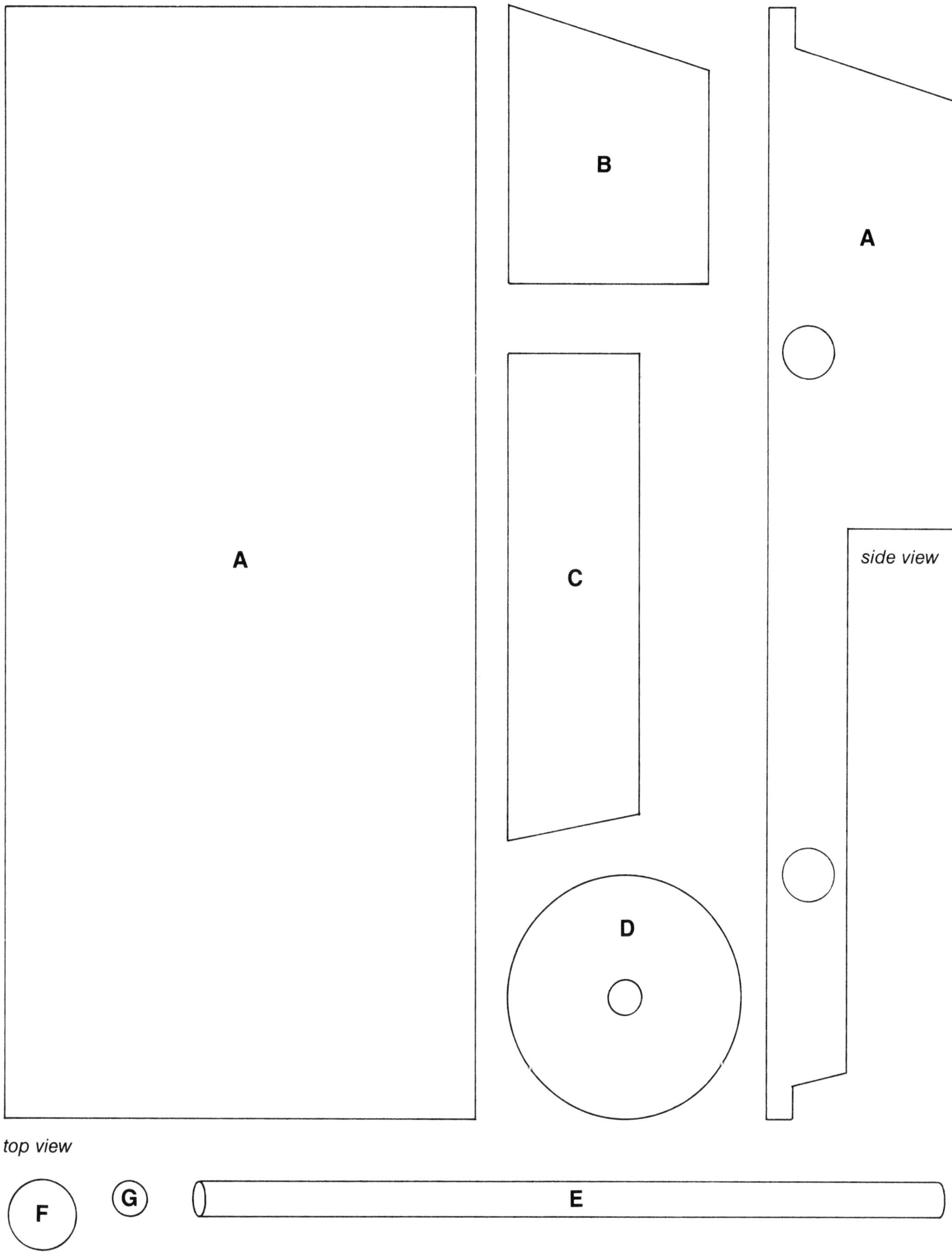

A

B

A

side view

C

D

top view

F

G

E

Plate 14

FIGHTER PLANE

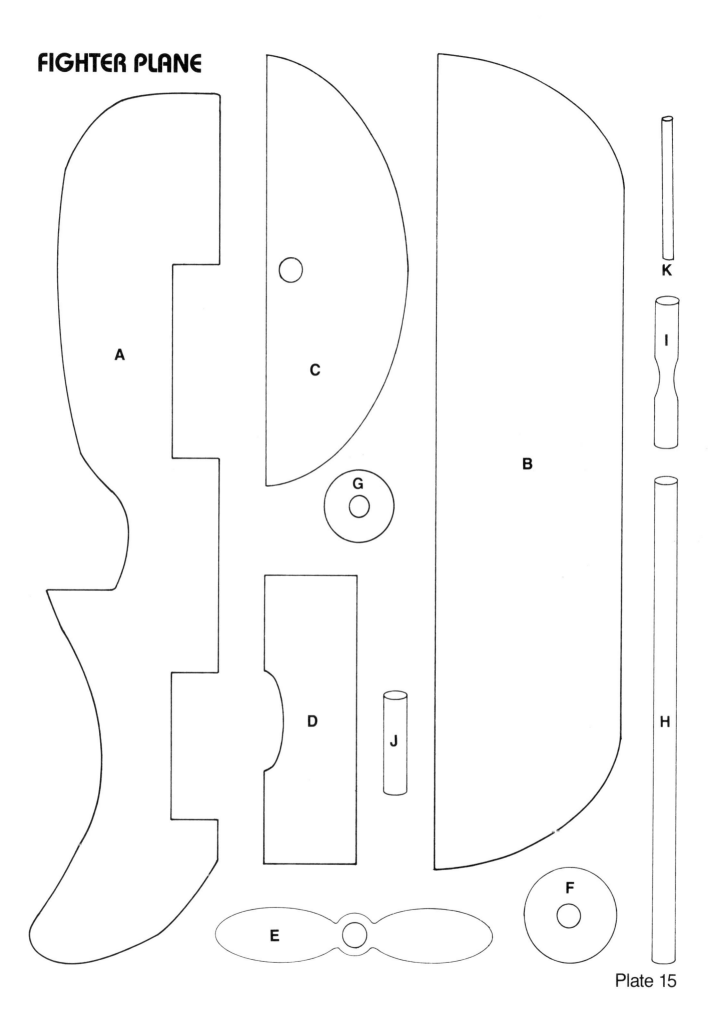

Plate 15

1	2	3	4	5	6	7	8	9	10
11	12	13	14	15	16	17	18	19	20
21	22	23	24	25	26	27	28	29	30
31	32	33	34	35	36	37	38	39	40
41	42	43	44	45	46	47	48	49	50
51	52	53	54	55	56	57	58	59	60
61	62	63	64	65	66	67	68	69	70
71	72	73	74	75	76	77	78	79	80
81	82	83	84	85	86	87	88	89	90
91	92	93	94	95	96	97	98	99	100
101	102	103	104	105	106	107	108	109	110
111	112	113	114	115	116	117	118	119	120
121	122	123	124	125	126	127	128	129	130
131	132	133	134	135	136	137	138	139	140
141	142	143	144	145	146	147	148	149	150
151	152	153	154	155	156	157	158	159	160
161	162	163	164	165	166	167	168	169	170
171	172	173	174	175	176	177	178	179	180
181	182	183	184	185	186	187	188	189	190
191	192	193	194	195	196	197	198	199	200
201	202	203	204	205	206	207	208	209	210
211	212	213	214	215	216	217	218	219	220
221	222	223	224	225	226	227	228	229	230
231	232	233	234	235	236	237	238	239	240
241	242	243	244	245	246	247	248	249	250
251	252	253	254	255	256	257	258	259	260
261	262	263	264	265	266	267	268	269	270
271	272	273	274	275	276	277	278	279	280
281	282	283	284	285	286	287	288	289	290
291	292	293	294	295	296	297	298	299	300
301	302	303	304	305	306	307	308	309	310
311	312	313	314	315	316	317	318	319	320
321	322	323	324	325	326	327	328	329	330
331	332	333	334	335	336	337	338	339	340
341	342	343	344	345	346	347	348	349	350
351	352	353	354	355	356	357	358	359	360
361	362	363	364	365	366	367	368	369	370
371	372	373	374	375	376	377	378	379	380
381	382	383	384	385	386	387	388	389	390
391	392	393	394	395	396	397	398	399	400